FACE TO FACE WITH
PENGUINS

By Yva Momatiuk
and John Eastcott

NATIONAL
GEOGRAPHIC
WASHINGTON, D.C.

FACE TO FACE

Our rubber boat rammed through a powerful surf and climbed a gravel beach. My husband, John, and I jumped out. We dragged the dinghy up the slope. If it floated out to sea, we could not return to *Golden Fleece,* the sailboat we came on, now 200 yards (183 m) away, bobbing on its anchor.

I grabbed my cameras and walked down the beach. After years of dreaming and planning, I was on South Georgia, a 100-mile-long (161 km) island

ARE PENGUINS TOO LAZY TO FLY?

Millions of years ago, there were prehistoric penguins. They evolved from birds that flew. Eventually, they became flightless full-time swimmers. Some prehistoric penguins were over six feet tall and weighed over 200 pounds (91 kg).

▬ Penguins fly under water! They use their wings (called flippers) to push their bodies forward.

▬ They swim many miles, chasing the small aquatic animals that they eat.

▬ Birds that fly have light, hollow bones. Penguins have solid bones, and they are heavier. This helps penguins dive and stay under water for long periods.

with a lofty spine of wild mountains and glaciers glistening like huge diamonds. I zipped up my parka. Even in summer the island was licked by the icy breath of the Antarctic continent, 900 miles (1,400 km) to the south.

I was not alone. A group of strangers in what looked like white shirts, dark jackets, and orange neck scarves came out of the sea toward me. They wobbled from side to side, their arms outstretched in a big welcome. King penguins, tall, slick, beautiful birds, were coming to greet me!

The birds stopped a few feet away, craning their long necks to inspect me. Trying not to scare them, I sat on the beach. Soon, they came even closer. It was a real face-to-face encounter! They were peering into my eyes curiously, as if asking, "Are you okay?" I assured them I was fine and very happy.

After a while I got cold, so I got up for a quick walk to warm up. Thousands of king penguins were everywhere, diving into the sea in noisy groups or standing together and moving their heads and wings as if talking to one another. I found some birds snoozing on gravel and

lay down among them on my stomach.

I stayed there, listening to them. They sounded like brass trumpets and buzzing bees. Suddenly, something touched my back. I held my breath and felt a pair of soft feet climbing on top of my body and walking around, exploring the new blue object on the beach. The penguin soon hopped off and waddled away, its curiosity satisfied.

My curiosity about these amazing birds was just beginning. I was impatient to learn all I could about them.

A group of king penguins with snowy white bellies, golden orange necks, and black heads comes out of the surf to greet me.

7

MEET

Two chinstrap penguins quarrel noisily, possibly trying to defend their space on the ice. Their stiff tail feathers help them not fall backward.

THE PENGUIN

A group of Adélie penguins rests on a small iceberg in the great polar landscape of ice, sea, and sky near the Antarctic Peninsula.

Penguins look like funny little men in tuxedos. They walk like us, upright. They spend much of their lives feeding in the sea, coming on land to raise their chicks.

Penguins are tough waterbirds. They can survive in some of the harshest places on Earth. They swim in punishing storms, battling surf and sharp ice to get to coastal rocks. They climb steep snowfields. They jump from boulders and dive in the freezing sea.

The oceans south of the equator shaped their

Chinstrap penguins dive under a small iceberg to chase tiny crustaceans called krill. Meanwhile, other birds use the ice as their floating perch.

bodies and life cycles. Look at their big marine home on the map on page 29. The land areas where penguins go to have their chicks are fairly small. The rest is all deep blue ocean, warmer near the equator and rapidly cooling toward the South Pole.

Almost all penguins live in cooler parts of the Southern Hemisphere. The largest, the emperor, breeds primarily in Antarctica. The next largest,

the king, breeds on nearby islands. The icy cold water is rich with the aquatic life that feeds these penguins and other birds, fish, seals, and whales.

One summer we watched two courting king penguins. We called them Maude and Albert, but since they looked the same, we were not sure which was which.

They joined 100,000 other birds on the beach.

⬆ *Royal penguins slide along a muddy trail on Macquarie Island, south of Australia. It is windy, wet, and chilly here, but warm enough for lush plants to grow.*

This area, called a rookery, is where penguins lay their eggs and the chicks are born and raised. It looked like a huge city, packed with tall, elegant kings. With a peck from their sharp bills, the penguins kept other kings out of their territory. The mates took turns and incubated their single white eggs on their feet for about 55 days. They kept the eggs warm in special brooding pouches on their lower bellies. Albert cared for the egg. Maude waddled away to fish.

Soon their chick hatched. She made funny peeping noises, so we called her Peepa. She huddled under her mom's or dad's warm belly. To feed her, Maude or Albert would vomit up fish they had partly digested. They took turns delivering bellyfuls of the fish mush into her open beak.

Peepa soon joined the other downy brown chicks. These groups, called crèches, looked like big nursery

A gentoo parent feeds its two fat chicks at the same time. To feed their young, parents bring up food from their bellies that has already been partly digested.

schools. Parents left to fish, bringing back food to the chicks. But once winter arrived, the parents would leave the chicks, sometimes for months. Peepa got hungry and lost weight. But Maude and Albert returned in spring. They recognized Peepa's whistle among thousands of others. They fed her until she could go to sea and fish for herself.

PENGUIN TALK!

Different species of penguins make different sounds. They honk, whistle, trumpet, buzz, bark, huff, quack, and growl. Each penguin also has its own unique voice. This helps penguins find their mates and chicks in a big crowd.

Penguin sounds belong to three main groups:

— Territorial: "I want to keep this spot to myself, so get lost!"

— Contact: "Hello, is that you?"

— Pair bonding: "I like you—do you like me, too?"

13

PENGUINS ROCK!

Imagine you are a penguin, diving in the cold Antarctic waters and looking for food. If the small fish and squid that you eat are hard to find, you will need to dive deeper. If you are an emperor penguin, you can stay under water for about 20 minutes to catch your food before you must come up for air.

You can survive this dive because your body has many built-in adaptations. You can't breathe under water, but you use oxygen stored in your body. Your heart rate can go from its usual 60-70 beats a minute down to 20 beats a minute. Some parts of your body, like your kidneys, nearly shut down so they use less oxygen. Your solid bones help you dive.

On your way up, you see a ferocious leopard seal hunting for a fat and tasty penguin to eat. You swim away, and this time you are lucky, and escape.

Penguins have a hard life, but their adaptations

Swimming for his life, a penguin tries to escape a large leopard seal.

help them survive. They see well under water, so they can chase their prey and spot any approaching danger. The colors of their feathers also help them hide in plain sight. Their dark backs (when seen from above) and their white bellies (when seen from below) make them hard to see in the sea. This can save their lives when predators like leopard seals or killer whales are chasing them.

They use different adaptations when they come ashore. The ice on coastal rocks might be hanging above their heads, but they have no hands to help them scramble up. So they pop out of the water like rockets and use their sharp claws to climb up the ice slope. They use their tails and spread their flippers in tricky places to catch their balance.

Now they are dripping wet, and it is cold and windy, but there is no sheltered place to get warm. Their top layer of short feathers is well oiled and waterproof. The dense down underneath traps a layer of insulating air close to their bodies. They have layers of fat to help keep them warm. Their short and dense feathers must be kept clean to insulate them, so they wash in the sea. They groom their feathers with their bills, spreading

⬆ *Snowflakes settle on a king penguin chick (top). A king penguin's foot (bottom) has small bumps and long claws, which help the bird climb on slippery rocks.*

WHAT'S THE SCOOP ON PENGUIN POOP?

A penguin's poop can make a big mess! It squirts out in a stream about two feet long. To poop, penguins turn away from their own nests, but they might splatter the fellow next to them.

— Penguins' poop, or guano, changes color, depending on what they're eating.

— What's the most common color of penguin poop? Pink! It turns this color if they're eating mostly krill.

— Sometimes the poop is white! This means they're eating a lot of fish. If it's green, it means they cannot find any food and are starving.

waterproofing oil from a gland near the tail.

Penguins are great swimmers and may "porpoise" by leaping above the water to grab a quick breath. Such leaps do not slow them down, though. They can swim faster than a good hiker can walk. Traveling on ice, they sometimes "toboggan," or slide along on their bellies.

There are many different kinds of penguins, and they have many different adaptations. Scientists say there are anywhere from 16 to 20 species. There is a lot of diversity among the different species.

Emperors are the largest penguins. They are almost four feet tall (1 m) and weigh about 65 pounds (29 kg). Every year, they endure several months in the freezer that is the Antarctic. Emperors march many miles to find good stable ice to have their chicks. In the depth of winter, they huddle together and rotate their positions, taking turns getting warm in the heart of the pack. And they swim fast, up to eight miles per hour (13 kph).

Little blues are the smallest penguins. They are only one foot tall and weigh around two pounds (1 kg). They live on the coast of New Zealand or Australia, and seldom see any snow. They do not

↑ Once their big chicks on shore need less care, king penguin parents can enjoy a summer dip together.

← Three gentoos leap, or porpoise, out of the water to catch a quick breath.

1 *An Adélie penguin spreading its flippers* **2** *A macaroni penguin grooming* **3** *Rockhopper penguins huddling together* **4** *An elegant chinstrap*

penguin **5** *An emperor penguin tobogganing on ice* **6** *The endangered yellow-eyed penguin, in New Zealand* **7** *Little blue, the smallest of all penguins*

dive as deep as other penguins do. They rear their chicks in only two months. Galápagos penguins also don't see any ice. They survive the hot climate near the equator thanks to sea currents bringing cold water full of nutrients. They can mate for life, breed up to three times a year, and lay their eggs in caves or crevices.

Other species of penguins include the king, Adélie, chinstrap, macaroni, royal, white-flippered, and gentoo. Then there are the Magellanic, Humboldt, African, yellow-eyed, Fiordland, Snares, erect-crested, and rockhopper (southern, northern, and eastern). Do you think you can remember them all?

21

This soaking-wet Adélie chick has not yet grown the layer of feathers that will help it repel water. It could freeze to death. Because of climate change, some penguin habitats now get more rain and snow in summer.

MARINE SENTINELS

A noisy city of king penguin chicks and adults, walking among huge southern elephant seals on the beach. Elephant seals usually do not hurt penguins.

Penguins are our marine sentinels. The word "sentinel" means a guard or a lookout, someone who warns us when something is wrong. Can birds tell us anything? Yes, they can, and some scientists are watching penguins closely.

Every year, millions of penguins breed on the same beaches and islands they used before. But some of these habitats are starting to change. This makes it harder to find food or causes the ice to retreat. Soon, the colony gets smaller. Sometimes it even disappears.

*A rainbow arches above
thousands of king penguins.*

The Earth is getting warmer. We call it climate change, or global warming. This change is caused by gases in the atmosphere that trap heat on Earth. We produce these gases by burning oil and coal to power our cars and planes, to heat and light our houses, and to run our factories.

As the Earth warms, so do the oceans. Fish, krill, and squid, which penguins eat, move away or seek deeper, colder water. Parent birds must swim much farther to fish, often too far to feed their chicks well.

Ships dump and spill oil and other chemicals, polluting the oceans and killing the birds. Commercial fishing vessels compete with penguins for fish and krill. In some penguin habitats, humans introduced dogs, ferrets, and other animals, which kill the birds.

If we do not protect penguins and their ecosystems, more species could become endangered. Let's work together to learn more about how to save penguins' habitats and help them thrive.

HOW YOU CAN HELP

▼ *This road sign in New Zealand warns drivers to watch out for penguins. In more populated areas, penguins are sometimes run over by cars.*

Penguins charm us with their comical bodies and waddling walk. But they are in trouble and need our protection. Because they breed on land in many countries, we need wise international efforts to save them. But there is a lot you can do right at home.

The dangers affecting penguins are very real. Emperor penguins, such as those shown in the 2005 film *March of the Penguins,* could be in trouble because the ice they live on is starting to disappear. This is in part due to global warming.

You can help fight global warming. These greenhouse gases come from the energy we all use, including electricity produced by coal-burning plants. There are lots of ways to use less energy.

▬ Oil drilling and oil spills hurt penguins and their habitat. The oil is used in the gasoline that our cars burn. If we drive less often, they might drill less. Plus, the gasoline fumes contribute to global warming. Help your family drive less. If your school or a friend's house is less than a mile away, ask someone in your family to walk you there rather than drive you. It will be good for your health and good for the planet, and it's fun. If it's too far to walk, maybe you can carpool with a friend or take public transportation.

▬ Help your family change all the traditional light bulbs in your home to energy-saving compact fluorescent bulbs.

▬ Use less plastic. Drink tap water. Fill a sports bottle instead of buying water in plastic bottles.

▬ See *March of the Penguins* and the animated movie *Happy Feet* to learn more about these amazing birds. Encourage your friends to see these films and learn all they can about penguins.

▬ You and your friends may like to "adopt" a penguin from National Wildlife Federation or World Wildlife Fund.

IT'S YOUR TURN

Learning about penguins may make you want to see them in person. You are in luck—you do not have to travel to the end of the world. Some excellent aquariums and zoos have small penguin colonies. There you can spend hours watching the birds waddling, hopping, calling out, feeding, and even diving.

For example, you can visit African penguins at the New England Aquarium in Boston, Massachusetts, or at the Monterey Bay Aquarium in Monterey, California. See Magellanic penguins at the Bronx Zoo in New York. Admire king penguins at the Saint Louis Zoo in Missouri.

Many of these parks also have webcams (video cameras) set up, so you can watch the birds right from home, on your computer. Type the name of the zoo or aquarium into your search engine to find the webcams. You can watch them and learn more about the birds.

There are no penguins in the wild in the United States, or in Canada or Mexico, our neighbors. But if you ever travel to South Africa, Australia, New Zealand, Chile, Argentina, the Galápagos Islands, or Antarctica, they will be waiting for you, welcoming you with open arms.

A pair of king penguins share a tender moment.

FACTS AT A GLANCE

⬇ *Deep footprints from a gentoo adult rushing to feed his chick in a snowy hilltop colony*

▬ Scientific Name

Penguins are birds that belong to the family Spheniscidae. Emperor penguins *(Aptenodytes forsteri)* were featured in the film *March of the Penguins*. Many of the pictures in this book are of the king penguin *(Aptenodytes patagonicus)*.

▬ Common Names

There are between 16 and 20 species of penguins. Common names are Adélie, African (also known as jackass or black-footed), chinstrap, emperor, erect-crested, Fiordland, Galápagos, gentoo, Humboldt, king, little blue (little, or fairy), macaroni, Magellanic, rockhopper (southern, northern, and eastern), royal, Snares, white-flippered, and yellow-eyed.

▬ Population

Macaroni and chinstrap penguins are the most numerous, with populations in the millions. In contrast, in 1999 scientists counted only 1,200 Galápagos penguins. Galápagos, northern rockhopper, erect-crested, and yellow-eyed pen-guins are listed as endangered by the International Union for Conservation of Nature and Natural Resources.

▬ Size

Emperors are the biggest penguins, with an average height of about 45 inches (115 cm) and an average weight of 65 pounds (29 kg). Little blue penguins are about 16 inches (40 cm) tall and weigh about 2 pounds (900 g).

▬ Lifespan

Many penguin chicks die before they are old enough to feed themselves. If a penguin makes it past the chick stage, it may live to be 15 to 20 years old.

▬ Special Features

Penguins' bones are unusually dense and heavy for birds. Unlike humans, penguins can drink seawater. They have glands near their eyes that help them get rid of the extra salt.

▬ Habitat

Penguins breed in the Southern Hemisphere. Many live close to Antarctica, but

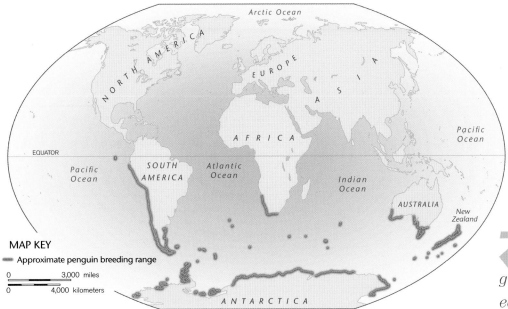

MAP KEY

Approximate penguin breeding range

| 0 | 3,000 miles |
| 0 | 4,000 kilometers |

Different species of penguins can be found from the equator to Antarctica.

others live closer to the equator. (People often think that polar bears and penguins live together, but they don't. Polar bears live way up north, in the Arctic.) Some penguins feed in the open ocean, while others feed in coastal waters. Adélie, emperor, rockhopper, and Magellanic penguins migrate. In fact, Magellanic penguins have been found to migrate more than 1,200 miles (2,000 km).

Food

Penguins eat small fish such as anchovies and sardines, krill, and squid.

Reproduction

One female usually pairs with one male for the season. The same male and female often pair up each year. Penguins lay eggs. The male and female share parenting duties of brooding (keeping the egg and chick warm) and feeding the chick until it is old enough to catch food for itself. King penguins need from 14 to 16 months to raise their chicks, longer than any other penguin species.

Biggest Threats

Oil companies drill for oil in the oceans near penguin habitats, and oil sometimes spills or leaks. Oil is poisonous to fish and other sea life. Every year, thousands of penguins die because they swallow or breathe in the oil. If the oil also coats their feathers, penguins freeze.

Global warming is causing the ice pack to disappear, so penguins have to move their breeding sites farther away. Plus, when warmer water replaces the cooler water, prey are harder to find.

Commercial fisheries harvest krill and small fish, so there is less food for the penguins to eat. In the water, penguins are preyed upon by leopard seals, sea lions, sharks, and killer whales.

GLOSSARY

Adaptations: gradual changes in an organism to make it function better in its environment

Aquatic: a word that describes birds and other organisms living in water

Critter: an informal term for a living creature

Dinghy: a small inflatable boat

Diversity: variations of life forms

Ecosystem: a natural unit of plants, animals, and microorganisms

Equator: imaginary line on the Earth's surface halfway between the North and South Poles, which divides it into Northern and Southern Hemispheres

Fossil fuels: carbons and hydro-carbons found in the Earth's crust

Gale: a very strong wind

Habitat: an area where certain birds, other animals, or plants live

Incubate: to sit on an egg to keep it warm so the chick can hatch

Krill: a small shrimp-like animal

Rookery: a colony of breeding penguins or other birds

Southern Hemisphere: the half of the planet that is south of the equator

Squid: a marine animal with eight arms

Tuxedo: a man's formal jacket, usually black

FIND OUT MORE

Books

Chester, Jonathan, and Patrick Regan. *Flipping Brilliant: A Penguin's Guide to a Happy Life.* New York, N.Y.: Andrews McMeel Publishing, 2008.

Fromental, Jean-Luc, and Joëlle Jolivet. *365 Penguins.* New York, N.Y.: Abrams Books for Young Readers, 2006.

Jacquet, Luc. *March of the Penguins: Companion to the Major Motion Picture.* Washington, D.C.: National Geographic Society, 2006.

Lynch, Wayne. *Penguins of the World.* New York, N.Y.: Firefly Books, 1999.

Sierra, Judy. *Antarctic Antics: A Book of Penguin Poems.* San Diego, Calif.: Harcourt Brace, 1998.

Simon, Seymour. *Penguins.* Washington, D.C.: Smithsonian, 2007.

Films

Happy Feet (2006), animated film directed by George Miller and Warren Coleman

March of the Penguins (2005), Academy Award winner in 2006 for best documentary feature

Madagascar (2005) computer-animated film produced by DreamWorks Animation

Web Sites

http://www.kidzone.ws/animals/penguins/index.htm

http://kids.nationalgeographic.com/Animals/CreatureFeature/Emperor-penguin/

http://community.clubpenguin.com/

http://www.surfnetkids.com/penguins.htm

http://tiki.oneworld.net/

http://www.penguinscience.com/education/postcards.php

http://www.penguinscience.com/classroom_home.php

RESEARCH & PHOTOGRAPHIC NOTES

To find penguins in the cold world of the Antarctic, we leave our house in the Catskills in New York and fly south. We cross the equator, reach the southern tip of South America, and fly east to the Falkland Islands. There we hop on Jerome Poncet's sailboat, called *Golden Fleece*, and our adventure begins.

As we sail, we sometimes see large tour boats. Some of them have heated pools, libraries, gyms, and more. But we prefer our small boat, which bounces a lot when the waves get big. We can slip into narrow bays or wiggle into a maze of grounded icebergs. When we explore, there are just a few of us, and we can hear the birds, the sea, and the wind. There is no TV on board, but we never miss it. The best National Geographic show is all around us, and we are living inside it rather than watching it.

When we get close to South Georgia, we start to feel the cold. Unlike penguins, we do not have oily feathers and a thick layer of fat. So we wear plenty of warm clothes—some that are windproof, some that are water resistant. And we wear hats! If anyone tells you that hats are stupid, do not believe it. We love our hats, and sometimes want to wear three of them at once. That's how cold it is!

Once we step ashore, John and I split up. We like to explore at our own pace, with our backpacks full of photographic equipment. But the land of the penguins can be dangerous. There are sudden gales whipping up the sea and making our return to *Golden Fleece* difficult. There are big waves striking the beach when our backs are turned. We get cold and tired. So we both carry walkie-talkies to stay in touch.

The neat part is always coming back to our small human community on the boat. It is evening, and the birds' voices outside sound clear and beautiful. We dig into our plates of hot food, tell stories about the penguins, and never tire of it.   —YM & JE

WE DEDICATE THIS BOOK TO
PENGUINS, WHEREVER THEY ARE.
—YM & JE

Acknowledgments

Our warmest thanks go to Jerome Poncet, explorer extraordinaire, and owner and skipper of *Golden Fleece,* the sailboat that carried us to South Georgia and Antarctica. Without his unsurpassed knowledge, generous help, advice, and enthusiasm, our work would not have been possible. We are grateful to Leiv Poncet for his masterful steering and landing of the dingy that took us ashore, and for all his help. To our great cook, Cathy Colle, we extend our special thanks. We miss her moonfish dishes, krill appetizers, mutton stew, and dandelion salads. We appreciate the assistance of Herman Niekamp, who over many years has built specialized photographic equipment for us. We thank Dr. David Ainley of W.T. Harvey and Associates for answering our many questions. And to our travel companions on three trips to penguin land, Shelley Gill, Beverly Davis, Diane Richardson, Richard Purington, Russ Gutshall, Fanus Weldhagen, Paul Souders, Hans Wolkers, Dan Paulson, Steve Kazlowsky, Tomek Gross, and Russ Allan: thanks, guys, for everything.

The publisher wishes to thank Dr. David Stokes, Associate Professor at the University of Washington, for his help with the map and text review.

Book design by David M. Seager. The body text of the book is set in ITC Century. The display text is set in Knockout and Party Noid.

Published by the
National Geographic Society

John M. Fahey, Jr., *President and Chief Executive Officer*

Gilbert M. Grosvenor, *Chairman of the Board*

Tim T. Kelly, *President, Global Media Group*

John Q. Griffin, *President, Publishing*

Nina D. Hoffman, *Executive Vice President; President, Book Publishing Group*

Staff for This Book

Nancy Laties Feresten, *Vice President, Editor-in-Chief of Children's Books*

Bea Jackson, *Design and Illustrations Director, Children's Books*

Amy Shields, *Executive Editor*

Mary Beth Oelkers-Keegan, *Project Editor*

David M. Seager, *Art Director*

Lori Epstein, *Illustrations Editor*

Marie McCarren, *Researcher*

Carl Mehler, *Director of Maps*

Sven M. Dolling, *Map Research and Production*

Jennifer Thornton, *Managing Editor*

Grace Hill, *Associate Managing Editor*

R. Gary Colbert, *Production Director*

Lewis R. Bassford, *Production Manager*

Nicole Elliott, *Manufacturing Manager*

Susan Borke, *Legal and Business Affairs*

Hardcover: 978-1-4263-0561-0
Library edition: 978-1-4263-0562-7

Front cover: Face to face with a chinstrap penguin; *front flap:* A curious king penguin checks out our camera; *back cover:* A group of king penguins marches back to the rookery; Yva Momatiuk and John Eastcott; *page one:* A Macaroni penguin leaps into the book; *pages 2–3:* King penguins in a rookery.